To Everly

Merry Christmas!.

Love,
Gre-Gred Shen-Shen

Books by Kids
1021 Oak Street
Jacksonville, FL 32204
www.booksbykids.com

Text by Paige McDowell

Editing and Design by Books by Kids

Illustrations by patients from Wake Forest Baptist Health Brenner Children's Hospital in Winston-Salem, NC

ISBN: 978-0-9830954-3-9
Printed in India

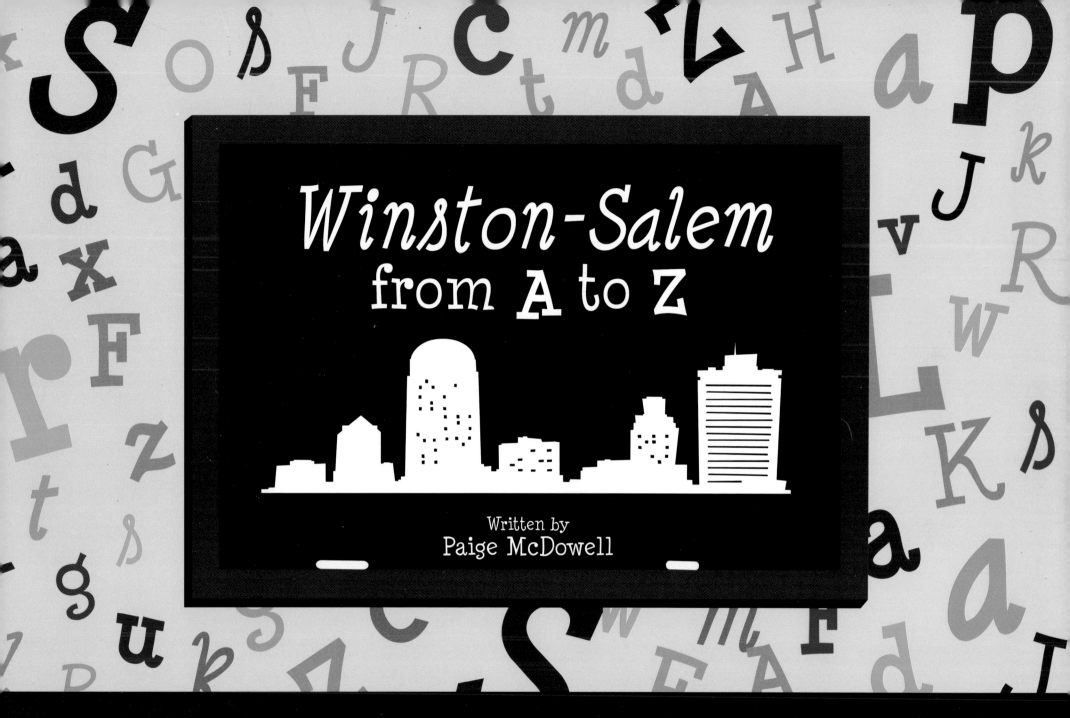

Winston-Salem
from **A** to **Z**

Written by
Paige McDowell

Illustrated by the amazing young patients of Wake Forest Baptist Health
Brenner Children's Hospital, which benefits from sales proceeds

The Bunn family dedicates this book to the memory and life of Jenny Kimbrel Bunn.

Special thanks to the Bunn family and Charlie Hemrick
for making this book possible.

About Wake Forest Baptist Health Brenner Children's Hospital

Founded in 1986, Brenner Children's Hospital is the only full-service pediatric hospital serving western North Carolina, providing expert care for neonates through teens in a state-of-the-art, 160-bed facility. We have more than 140 pediatricians specializing in over 30 areas of pediatric medicine. As North Carolina's only Level 1 Pediatric Trauma Center, Brenner Children's Pediatric Emergency Department is staffed 24 hours a day by pediatric specialists. From research into childhood diseases, to the latest diagnostic technologies, treatments and surgical techniques—many of which are only found at Brenner Children's—we are committed to advancing pediatric care and training not only locally, but worldwide.

What makes this book so special?

Wake Forest®
Baptist Health
Brenner Children's Hospital

This book was written by children, for children. With each word, splash of color, and brushstroke, *Winston-Salem from A to Z* highlights the many things that local children love about the place they call home!

The Friends of Brenner Children's Hospital and the Books by Kids Foundation sponsored the Brenner Young Authors Contest to give all middle school students in Forsyth County an opportunity to compete to author *Winston-Salem from A to Z*. All participating students were given an A to Z starter list containing local venues, characteristics, and historic figures that correspond to each letter of the alphabet. Students were encouraged to use the list as a guide to write a unique story about Winston-Salem. After reviewing several creative entries, a panel of judges selected Paige McDowell's story as the winner, and she received a Kindle Fire and a pizza party!

The colorful illustrations were created by talented patients at Wake Forest Baptist Health Brenner Children's Hospital. Thanks to our sponsors, all sales proceeds will be donated to patient programs at Brenner, thus benefiting our young patients for years to come!

About Books by Kids

Winston-Salem from A to Z is part of the A to Z Series, published and designed by Books by Kids. All books in the series are educational in nature, benefit non-profit organizations, and are illustrated and written in part by children. For more information, visit booksbykids.com.

Books by Kids .com ®

Winston-Salem is my town,

there's much to do and see!

We'll go through the whole alphabet,

so come explore with me.

A is for the *Air Show*,
that comes just once a year.
Helicopters, fighter planes,
and pilots in their gear!

A famous Deacon that we know
achieved great golfing fame.
He went to college in our town,
Arnold Palmer
is his name.

City of the Arts
is the nickname
of our city.
Museums, music,
drama, dance,
and galleries so pretty.

Abigail - age 8

Brenner Children's Hospital

Brenner Children's Hospital

is what begins with B.
With stellar nurses
and great docs
who care for you and me.

B also stands for *Bookmarks*,
a fun festival downtown.
Authors of great books are there,
they come from all around.

Heather – age 17

C is for Children's Museum

with eclectic art galore.
From a bright green giant beanstalk
to a mini grocery store.

A Moravian tradition
in Old Salem starts with C.
You'll learn about our heritage
at our festive *Candle Tea.*

The NBA's *Chris Paul*
is a star who grew up here.
With outstanding values,
he's a star we proudly cheer.

Carson - age 4

Dewey's is the place we go for fresh delicious treats. Cakes, baked breads, and cookies and a bunch of sinful sweets.

D stands for the *Dash*, our local baseball team. Their mascot's name is Bolt, he will really make you scream!

Molly - age 14

Dixie Classic starts with D, a fair we all adore. With rides, fun games, and candy, it will leave you wanting more.

Downtown is another D, old buildings all around. Honking horns, live music, and great nightlife all abound.

Easter Sunrise Service
draws friends from far and near.
We gather in Old Salem
and sing hymns for all to hear.

Victoria - age 11

E is for the fun Events that Brenner hosts each year.
The Brenner Walk and Bike Race is a new one we hold dear.

FARMERS MARKET

Festival of Lights starts with F, a Tanglewood attraction. People drive from miles around to see Christmas lights in action.

Our local *Farmer's Market* is an awesome F we know. Tomatoes, apples, greens, and beans and things our farmers grow.

Aleesia - age 5

The *Festival of Trees* we host each year is so much fun. With sparkling trees adorned with love, we cherish every one.

G is for *Greek Festival*

that kicks off in mid-May.

With yummy food and music,

time will quickly fade away.

Goody's Headache Powder was invented in our town. It will ease your throbbing head and keep you from feeling down.

G stands for *Graylyn,* an impressive grand estate.

With old-world charm, the home was once the largest in the state.

Isabella - age 8

Humane Society is an H that offers love and care
to poor, defenseless animals
with them our love we share.

Zachary - age 7

Hanes Mall is where you're sure to find
clothing, shoes, and toys.

The festive bright merry-go-round is fun for girls and boys.

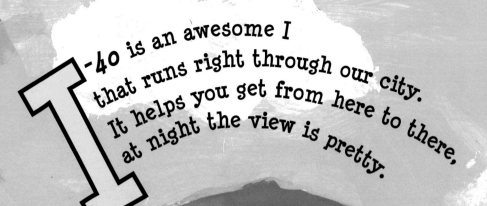

I-40 is an awesome I
that runs right through our city.
It helps you get from here to there,
at night the view is pretty.

I stands for *Industries*
that tell about our past.
Tobacco, textiles, furniture,
their impact has been vast.

I stands for *Innovation*.
We have proudly paved the way
for arts and business start ups
that enrich our lives each day.

Katie - age 7

Joseph Winston starts with J,
a war hero just the same.
His name is of importance here,
it's where Winston got its name.

Savannah - age 15

WORLD WAR II

The Lawrence Joel Coliseum
is a bustling J that's here.
It hosts great concerts, games, and shows
for local fans to cheer.

K is for a yummy snack we know as *Krispy Kreme*. The business got its start right here when the Rudolphs had a dream.

From jelly-filled to sprinkled tops, they're ever oh so sweet. Even the glazed original is such a tasty treat.

Madeleine - age 10

L is for the *Leaves* that change
and fall from every tree.
From deep dark browns to crimson reds,
it's quite a sight to see.

Anna - age 16

L stands for *Lovefeasts,*
a Moravian feast of love.
People sing their favorite hymns
and pray to God above.

N is for *UNCSA Nutcracker,*
a glorious sight to see.
Sugarplum fairies and
wicked mice
all dancing gracefully.

The *National Black Theatre Festival*
has become a huge showcase.
Musicians, actors, dancers all
perform with style and grace.

Katie - 13

O is for *Old Salem*,
a place that we hold dear.
With quaint boutiques
and houses,
in 1766 it started here.

Abigail - age 8

From Salem Tavern and Winkler Bakery to walks on cobblestone streets,
you'll learn about our past as you shop for fine antiques.

P is for our great *Parades*,
which truly are the best.
Christmas, Veteran's, Homecoming
all stand out from the rest.

Parks also start with P,
where we kids love to play.

Biking, baseball, playing catch
are great ways to spend the day!

Sydney - age 8

Q

is for our
Quality of Life,
in Winston
it's so grand!

With friendly
neighbors
all around,
we're the nicest
in the land!

Patricia - age 18

Reynolda House starts with R,
'twas RJ Reynolds' home from the start.
It's now a grand museum
of magnificent American art.

We also have a famous R,
the *Reynolds Building* is its name.
The Empire State Building came from it,
since New York wanted the same.

Linn - age 7

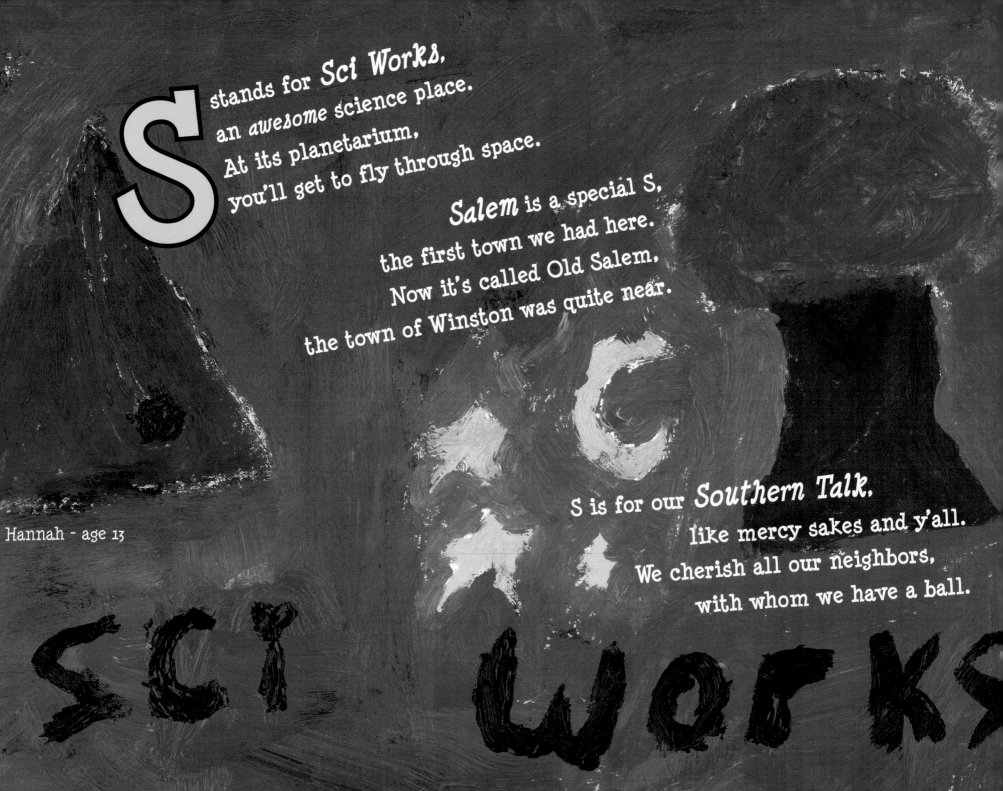

S stands for *Sci Works,*
an *awesome* science place.
At its planetarium,
you'll get to fly through space.

Salem is a special S,
the first town we had here.
Now it's called Old Salem,
the town of Winston was quite near.

S is for our *Southern Talk,*
like mercy sakes and y'all.
We cherish all our neighbors,
with whom we have a ball.

Hannah - age 13

Tanglewood starts with T,
a park with many things.
Ride a horse, go camping, or just
have fun on the swings!

Texas Pete has 2 T's and has become well known.
From Original to Chipotle, the business here was grown.

Madeleine - age 10

U stands for Universities,
we have several good ones here.
They'll fill your mind with knowledge
to help you land a great career.

Sara - age 17

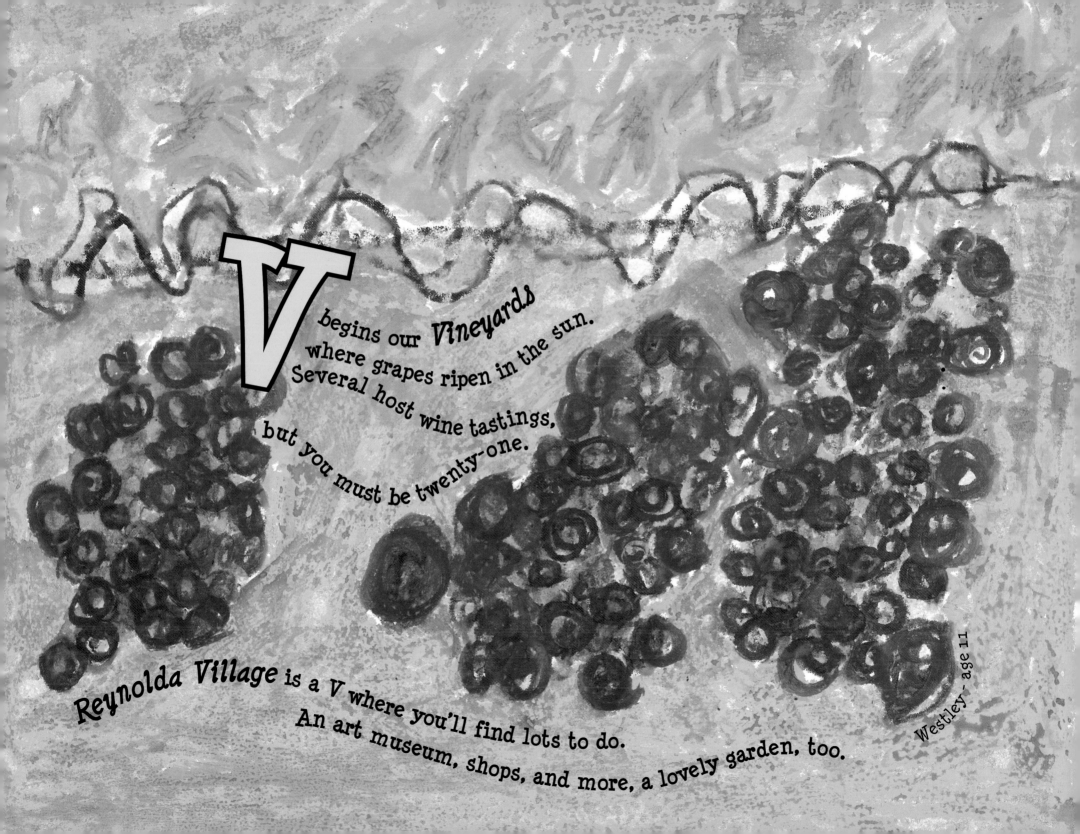

V begins our *Vineyards*
where grapes ripen in the sun.
Several host wine tastings,
but you must be twenty-one.

Reynolda Village is a V where you'll find lots to do.
An art museum, shops, and more, a lovely garden, too.

Westley - age 11

W is for *Wake Forest*
with colors black and gold.
Cheering on the Demon Deacons
is such fun for young and old.

With football in the fall
and soccer in the spring,
Wake Forest University
has a bit of everything.

Herme - age 11

X

marked the spot in '13
down on Cherry Street.
Winston and Salem merged to form
a town that can't be beat.

Marshall - age 10

Y stands for *Yadkin River,*
through our county does it flow.
Supplying us with water
that helps plants and bodies grow.

Aleesia – age 5

Z is for the *Zevely Inn*,
a historic place to stay.
Enjoy the sights and then relax
as you end a
fun-filled day.

Hannah - age 12

Tiberius - age 11

Juan Carlos - age 5

Emma - age 5

Daniel - age 5

WF

That's it for this A to Z,

from the present to the past.

I hope you've learned about our town,

and that you've had a blast!

How much do you know about Winston-Salem? Take the quiz below to find out!

1. In what year did Winston and Salem merge to form Winston-Salem?
   a. 1953
   b. 1913
   c. 1899
   d. 1933

2. How many times a year does the air show take place?
   a. five
   b. twice
   c. once

3. What is the nickname for Winston-Salem?
   a. City of Innovation
   b. City of Lights
   c. City of the Arts
   d. City of Agriculture

4. What is the name of our local baseball team's mascot?
   a. Dash
   b. Bolt
   c. Warthog

5. Where is the Candle Tea held?

6. Who lived in the Reynolda House?
   a. RJ Reynolds
   b. Abe Lincoln
   c. Ronald Reagan
   d. Bowman Gray

7. Old Salem dates back to:
   a. 1786
   b. 1776
   c. 1796
   d. 1766

8. For whom is the town of Winston named?
   a. Albert Salem
   b. Mildred Winston
   c. George Wilson
   d. Joseph Winston

9. What is the name of the doughnut company founded in our city?
   a. Krispy Donuts
   b. Dunkin Donuts
   c. Baskin Robbins
   d. Krispy Kreme

10. What interstate runs through our city?

11. When does the Greek Festival occur?
    a. July
    b. Mid-May
    c. End of March
    d. December 15th

12. What headache medicine was developed in Winston-Salem?
    a. Goody's Headache Powder
    b. Penicilin
    c. Hanes Insulin

13. What sauce was first made in Winston-Salem?
    a. Texas Piper
    b. Heinz Ketchup
    c. Texas Pete
    d. NC Heat

14. What is the name of our Children's Hospital?

Answers: 1. B 2. C 3. C 4. B 5. Old Salem 6. A 7. D 8. D 9. D 10. I-40 11. B 12. A 13. C 14. Brenner Children's Hospital

F is for the Friends of Brenner Children's Hospital

The Friends of Brenner Children's Hospital, established in 1987, is a group of dedicated volunteers who support the hospital through fundraising and community awareness activities. With more than 900 members, the Friends organize such annual events as Festival of Trees, Cheers! A toast to children's health, the 99.5WMAG Brenner Children's Hospital Radiothon, Brenner Walk and Bike Race, and the Celebrity Golf Classic.

Winston-Salem from A to Z was produced to commemorate the 25th anniversary of the Friends of Brenner Children's Hospital. Thank you for joining us in supporting children and ensuring they have access to the best health care available.

About the Author

Winston-Salem from A to Z was written by Paige McDowell, a 12-year-old sixth grader from Jefferson Middle School. Paige's love for creative writing began in elementary school and has continued ever since. Her favorite subject is Language Arts, where she is able to express her creativity. In her spare time, Paige enjoys bike riding, reading, drawing, and being with friends and family. She is a member of a local Girl Scout troop, as well as part of a travel soccer team where she likes to play defense. She lives in Winston-Salem with her mom, dad, younger brother, Drew, and her dog, Lucy. Paige would like to thank her sixth grade teachers for encouraging her to enter the A to Z writing contest and for inspiring her to strive for excellence.

About the Illustrators

The illustrations for *Winston-Salem from A to Z* were masterfully created by some amazing young people, all current or former patients at Brenner Children's Hospital. The illustrations were facilitated by staff members in the hospital's Child Life Department, the program director and volunteers of the Arts for Life program, and local elementary school art teacher, Randy Raines.

Arts for Life is a non-profit organization supporting people facing serious illnesses and disabilities. By providing educational visual arts, music and creative writing programs, Arts for Life enriches patients' lives, nurtures their minds and spirits, and encourages positive health care experiences for children and their families. Established at Brenner Children's Hospital, Arts for Life provides more than 65 hours a week of hands-on art projects to patients. Visit our website at aflnc.org.

arts for life

Special Thanks

Royce and Harriet Hough brought the idea of producing *Winston-Salem from A to Z* to the Friends of Brenner Children's Hospital and graciously served as the project's honorary chairmen.

Together, we thank the family of Jenny Kimbrel Bunn and Charlie Hemrick and the Sam N. Carter and Pauline H. Carter Fund of The Winston-Salem Foundation for generously supporting this project and making this book possible. Jenny lived life to the fullest and spent it volunteering with organizations to help children. Her family is very happy to dedicate this book in her memory. The family advisors to the Sam N. Carter and Pauline H. Carter Fund have focused their grantmaking on the health and education of children and families in the Winston-Salem community since 2000.

The Friends of Brenner Children's Hospital and the Books by Kids Foundation held the Brenner Young Authors Writing Contest to determine the author of *Winston-Salem from A to Z*. Several middle school students from Forsyth County submitted creative entries. Many thanks to our panel of community judges - Lynn Eisenberg, Friends of Brenner; Cameron Kent, WXII News 12; Annette Lynch, Winston-Salem Foundation; Royce Hough, Honorary Chair; and Dr. Marty Scott, Vice President of Brenner Children's Hospital - for evaluating the entries and helping to select the winning author. The decision was tough, indeed! Thank you to Paige McDowell for her entry and to her facilitator and mother, Michelle McDowell.

In addition to Paige, we want to recognize the other finalists who submitted wonderful entries: Sophie Davis of Redeemer School, Scott Campbell of East Forsyth Middle School, and Anna Hartley Anderson, who is home schooled. We extend special thanks to the students, their parents, teachers, and all others who supported participation in this project.

Finally, we want to thank Brenner Children's Hospital and the amazing children who illustrated each page of this book. Thank you to the hospital's Child Life department, the Arts for Life program, and local art teacher, Randy Raines, for their help in facilitating the illustrations.

We hope *Winston-Salem from A to Z* provides a fun way for children, young and old, to learn about our community for years to come. Its publication represents the collaborative support of community volunteers, children, and individuals who value our city and the vital care provided at Brenner Children's Hospital.